Trudie—
Happy Cooking!
The Stones "02"

vegetables

vegetables

VICKI LILEY

PERIPLUS

contents

vegetables

vegetables

With their abundance of varieties, and their vast array of colors, textures, and flavors, vegetables provide endless inspiration for cooks. The days of facing mushy, overcooked carrots or beans at the table have long vanished. Diners now crave the robust, earthy goodness of fresh vegetables and appreciate their essential role in every meal.

Take a trip to a well-stocked local market, and you'll be amazed at the choices: the crisp textures of Asian greens, the sweetness of red and orange bell peppers (capsicums), the delicate flavor of young fresh spinach and the fiery bite of chili peppers.

This is just a sampling of the produce used in this collection combining popular staples with vegetables that may be less familiar but are no less delicious. The 39 recipes rely on the freshest produce available, whether from a market or from your own garden. If you grow your own—or are fortunate enough to shop at a farmer's market—you well know the pleasure of biting into a fresh-picked, sun-ripened tomato or tasting the first forkful of salad made with just-harvested greens.

This book is not, strictly speaking, a vegetarian cookbook. Though the recipes do not use meat, fish or poultry, some include dairy products and eggs. Most of all, this is a celebration of the versatility of vegetables and the many ways they contribute to a meal.

There are sections devoted to mushrooms and to vegetable fruits such as tomatoes and eggplants. Other vegetables are classified by their edible parts: leaves and flowers, roots and tubers, pods and seeds, bulbs and squash, and stalks and shoots. Within these categories, you'll discover such delights as roasted tomatoes with garlic and lime, Jerusalem artichokes with spicy vegetables, baby beet salad with aioli, and cheese and zucchini fritters.

Experiment with varieties different from those you know, and you'll be rewarded with scrumptious vegetable creations.

Happy cooking!

Roasting bell peppers (capsicums)

1 Cut peppers in half through stem. Remove seeds and white pith. Place cut side down onto parchment-lined (baking paper–lined) baking sheets.

2 Bake at 425°F (220°C/Gas 7) or broil (grill) until skins are blistered and charred, about 15 minutes.

3 Place charred peppers in a plastic bag. Seal and allow to stand for 15 minutes.

4 Remove peppers from bag, then peel away and discard skins.

5 Place roasted pepper in a jar and cover with extra virgin olive oil. Seal and store in refrigerator. They will keep for 14 days.

Use in salads, sandwiches, pasta sauces and as part of an antipasto. (If oil solidifies in refrigerator, bring to room temperature.)

Chopping an onion

1 Halve onion lengthwise through root and stem ends.

2 Peel onion by removing outer layers of skin.

3 Slice through each onion half 3 or 4 times, parallel to cut surface, to within ½ inch (12 mm) of root end.

4 Slice 4 or 5 times through onion, without cutting into root end.

5 Finally, cut through previous cuts.

1

2

1

2

3

3

4

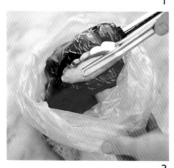

3

5

Preparing a globe artichoke

1 Hold artichoke firmly and bend stem back until it snaps from base. Alternatively, cut off with a knife.
2 Remove outer leaves by pulling each leaf away from artichoke and then downward to break tough upper part from leaf's fleshy base. Continue until you reach tender inner leaves, which are yellowish green in color.
3 Using a stainless steel knife, cut off one-third of artichoke top.
4 Rub cut surfaces with lemon juice to prevent discoloration.
5 Remove prickly choke with a teaspoon.
6 Place artichoke in bowl containing water and juice of 1 lemon.

Sautéing spinach leaves

1 Melt 1 tablespoon 1oz (30 g) butter in a frying pan over medium heat. Add crushed garlic to taste and cook for 1 minute.
2 Turn off heat, add washed spinach leaves and toss until coated in butter.
3 Cover and allow to stand for 2 minutes.
Serve immediately.

1

2

3

4

5

1

2

3

Removing corn from a fresh cob

1 Strip corn husks and silk down to stem end of corn.

2 Snap off husks and remove any remaining silk.

3 Grip stem firmly and use a sharp knife to slice away kernels. Slice close to woody cob.

Removing seeds from a tomato

1 Slice tomato in half through stem.

2 Remove seeds, using a teaspoon.

1

2

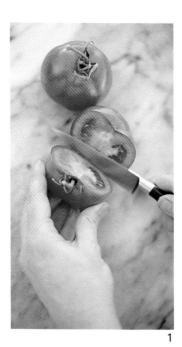

1

2

3

Peeling a tomato

To peel a tomato remove the core, cut a small cross in bottom of tomato, barely piercing skin. Drop tomato into boiling water, about 10 seconds for a ripe tomato and slightly longer for a firm tomato. Remove from water. Skin will come off easily.

Shelling and peeling fava (broad) beans

1 Press down on curved side of pod, and pull pod open. Run your thumb down length of pod to expose beans. Remove beans and discard pod.

2 Peel each bean, using your thumbnail to split opaque skin at the bean's tip. Pull skin carefully away from bean.

Removing seeds from a bell pepper (capsicum)

1 If recipe requires a whole pepper, slice top off with a sharp knife. If not, cut bell pepper in half through stem.

2 Using your fingers, remove and discard seeds and white pith from inside pepper.

1

2

1

2

Stir-frying vegetables

1 Heat 2 tablespoons oil in a wok or large frying pan over high heat. Add sliced vegetables such as asparagus, Asian greens (bok choy, choy sum and Chinese cabbage) and bell pepper (capsicum).

2 Fry, stirring and tossing constantly, until vegetables are tender–crisp, 2–3 minutes.
Serve immediately.

Preparing thick asparagus

1 If asparagus spears are thick and woody, peeling away tough skin from stalk will result in more tender asparagus after cooking.

2 Using a vegetable peeler or sharp knife, peel away a thin layer of skin beginning at lower part of stem, tapering off progressively as skin becomes more tender toward tip.

Wilting spinach leaves

1 Remove spinach roots.

2 Wash leaves and place in a colander or strainer over a heatproof bowl or saucepan.

3 Pour boiling water over leaves until they just begin to wilt and their color intensifies.
Serve immediately.

Chopping fresh herbs

1 Use sharp kitchen shears to snip fresh herbs.

This section offers a rainbow of vegetables: green, red and yellow sweet peppers, purple-skinned eggplants (aubergines), bright red tomatoes and avocados with their pebbly, dark-green skin and tender, light-green flesh.

While all vegetable fruits combine well with other foods and with one another, none matches the tomato for versatility. It can be enjoyed raw or cooked, used as the main ingredient in a recipe or as an addition that complements a recipe's other ingredients. The tomato features in an endless number of dishes from almost every national cuisine. The best-tasting specimens are those allowed to ripen on the vine. Once ripe, tomatoes should be stored at room temperature for no more than a day, then kept in the refrigerator.

Eggplants have mildly sweet, pale flesh and skin that ranges from mauve and purple to nearly black. Some have skins that are white or green. Asian eggplants are elongated; globe eggplants are more rotund. Store eggplants in the vegetable crisper of the refrigerator for up to five days.

There are hundreds of sweet peppers and chili peppers, with almost as many variations in size, shape, color and flavor, from large, mild bell peppers (capsicums) to small, fiery chili peppers. Red, green and yellow bell peppers can be used interchangeably in many recipes, though they differ slightly in taste. The red variety is simply the green pepper left on the vine to ripen. It has a sweeter, mellower flavor than the green. Another variety turns bright yellow when ripe instead of red.

Although available year-round, chili peppers are more plentiful at the height of summer. Generally, the smaller the chili, the more powerful the heat. Color is not an indication of pungency, with small green chilis sometimes more potent than red ones. When handling chili peppers, don't touch your face or eyes, and always wash your hands thoroughly afterward.

Store sweet bell peppers in the vegetable crisper of the refrigerator for up to five days. Chili peppers are best wrapped in a paper towel and stored in the vegetable crisper for up to ten days.

The avocado, like the tomato, is a fruit that for centuries has been consumed as a vegetable. For many avocado aficionados, the classic way to eat this fruit is to pit and peel it and brush the cut surfaces with fresh lime or lemon juice and serve it with salad or make it into guacamole. Purchase an avocado just before it is completely ripe, as the mature fruit has a short shelf life. Once ripe, an avocado may be held for one or two days in the refrigerator. To ripen a firm avocado, place in a paper bag and let stand at room temperature.

Salad-filled tomatoes

8 medium vine-ripened tomatoes

$1/2$ red (Spanish) onion

$1/2$ green bell pepper (capsicum), seeds removed

$1/2$ English (hothouse) cucumber, seeds removed

$3^{1}/2$ oz (105 g) good-quality firm feta cheese

8 black olives

1 teaspoon dried oregano

2 tablespoons extra virgin olive oil

1 tablespoon red wine vinegar

freshly ground black pepper to taste

Using a sharp knife, slice tops off tomatoes, reserving tops. Remove and discard tomato seeds and pulp using a teaspoon. Cut onion into thin wedges. Julienne (cut into matchstick lengths pepper, cucumber and feta. Combine onion, pepper, cucumber, feta and olives in a bowl. Place oregano, olive oil, vinegar and pepper in a screw-top jar. Shake well to combine. Pour over vegetables and gently toss to coat. Spoon filling into tomato shells.

Serve with reserved tomato tops.

Makes 8

SALAD-FILLED TOMATOES

Grilled eggplant on bruschetta with tomato salsa

1 medium eggplant (aubergine)

sea salt

6 thick slices wood-fired bread (if unavailable,
  use rustic or country loaf)

3 tablespoons olive oil

2 cloves garlic, halved

FOR TOMATO SALSA

2 medium tomatoes, chopped

$1/2$ red (Spanish) onion, chopped

2 tablespoons chopped fresh flat-leaf parsley

1 tablespoon balsamic vinegar

2 teaspoons extra virgin olive oil

freshly ground black pepper to taste

Cut eggplant crosswise into 8 thin slices, discarding stem and bottom. Place slices in a colander or strainer and sprinkle with salt. Allow to stand until eggplant begins to sweat, about 30 minutes.

To make tomato salsa: In a small bowl, combine all ingredients. Mix well. Cover and allow to stand 10 minutes before serving.

Rinse eggplant well under cold water to remove salt. Pat dry with paper towels.

Preheat a broiler (grill). Brush bread slices, on both sides, with 2 tablespoons olive oil and broil (grill) until golden, 1–2 minutes per side. Remove from heat, then brush each slice with a little more olive oil. Rub with garlic.

Brush eggplant slices with oil and broil (grill) until golden, 1–2 minutes per side.

Place bruschetta on warm serving plates, and top each with 2 eggplant slices. Spoon tomato salsa over eggplant and serve immediately.

Serves 4

Hint

A wood or gas barbecue can also be used to prepare bread.

GRILLED EGGPLANT ON BRUSCHETTA

Avocados with strawberry vinaigrette

8 oz (250 g) strawberries, hulls removed

2 tablespoons olive oil

3 tablespoons lemon juice

1 teaspoon superfine (caster) sugar

freshly ground black pepper to taste

2 ripe avocados

green leaves, for garnish

Place strawberries, olive oil, 2 tablespoons lemon juice, sugar and pepper in a food processor. Process until a thick sauce forms, about 30 seconds. Transfer to a pitcher, cover and refrigerate until ready to serve.

Slice each avocado in half through stem. Peel away outer skin and remove pit. Brush cut surfaces with remaining lemon juice.

Place avocado halves on serving plates. Top with dressing and garnish with fresh green leaves from your garden.

Serves 4

Hint

Green leaves such as flat-leaf parsley, rosemary, sage and mint may be used for garnish.

AVOCADOS WITH STRAWBERRY VINAIGRETTE

Spinach- and egg-filled peppers

4 medium red bell peppers (capsicums)

3 tablespoons vegetable oil

1 clove garlic, crushed

1 onion, chopped

7 oz (220 g) spinach leaves, shredded

1 teaspoon chopped fresh thyme

4 eggs

freshly ground black pepper to taste

Preheat oven to 350°F (180°C/Gas 4). Using a sharp knife, slice tops off bell peppers and reserve. Using your fingers, remove and discard seeds and white pith from bell peppers. Trim flesh from around pepper tops and finely chop.

Warm oil in a frying pan over medium heat. Add garlic and onion and cook until softened, about 2 minutes. Add chopped pepper, spinach and thyme and cook, stirring gently, until spinach has wilted, about 5 minutes. Divide spinach mixture among peppers, leaving a slight well in center for an egg.

Place filled peppers in an ovenproof dish, arranging them fairly closely together. Pour ½ cup (4 fl oz/125 ml) boiling water in dish and cover loosely with aluminum foil. Cook until peppers are soft when pierced with a skewer, 15–20 minutes. Remove from oven, lift foil and break an egg in well of each pepper. Cover again with foil, return to oven and bake until eggs are set, 10–15 minutes.

Serve hot, sprinkled with pepper.

Serves 4

Hint

Choose bell peppers (capsicums) with even bottoms

so they do not tip during cooking.

SPINACH- AND EGG-FILLED PEPPERS

Eggplant and mozzarella sandwiches

2 medium eggplants (aubergines)

sea salt

1 cup (4 oz/125 g) dried breadcrumbs

2 tablespoons freshly grated parmesan cheese

1 tablespoon chopped fresh flat-leaf parsley

3 tablespoons olive oil

5 oz (150 g) mozzarella, cut into $1/16$-inch
  (2-mm) slices

2 eggs, beaten

green leaves such as olive tree leaves, for garnish

Preheat oven to 350°F (180°C/ Gas 4). Cut eggplant crosswise into ½-inch (12-mm) rounds. Place slices in a colander or strainer and sprinkle liberally with salt. Allow to stand until eggplant begins to sweat, about 30 minutes. Rinse eggplant well under cold water to remove salt. Pat dry with paper towels.

In a small bowl, combine breadcrumbs, parmesan and parsley. Mix well.

Pour olive oil in a shallow baking pan and warm in oven for 5 minutes, then remove from oven.

Sandwich a mozzarella slice between 2 eggplant slices. Dip eggplant sandwich in beaten egg, then in breadcrumb mixture. Place sandwiches in pan in a single layer.

Bake for 15 minutes. Turn sandwiches and cook until golden, about 15 minutes. Remove from oven and drain on paper towels.

Slice each sandwich in half and garnish with green leaves.

Serves 3–4

Hints

Serve sandwiches with a tossed green salad. If olive tree leaves are unavailable, substitute flat-leaf parsley, rosemary or sage leaves.

EGGPLANT AND MOZZARELLA SANDWICHES

Roasted tomatoes with garlic and lime

16 small vine-ripened tomatoes

juice of 2 limes

2 teaspoons Asian sesame oil

2 cloves garlic, crushed

2 tablespoons balsamic vinegar

1 teaspoon sea salt

cracked black pepper to taste

sea salt, for serving

baby arugula (rocket) leaves, for serving

lime wedges, for serving

Preheat oven to 225°F (110°C/Gas ¼). Using a sharp knife, cut 2 shallow slits in any part of each tomato. Place tomatoes on a parchment-lined (baking paper–lined) baking sheet. In a small bowl, combine lime juice, sesame oil, garlic and vinegar. Drizzle over tomatoes. Sprinkle with salt and plenty of black pepper.

Bake tomatoes for 1 hour. Turn oven off and allow tomatoes to cool in oven, about 1 hour. Carefully transfer to a serving dish.

Serve accompanied with sea salt, arugula leaves and lime wedges.

Serves 6–8

Hint

The tomatoes can be stored, covered, in the refrigerator for up to 3 days.

ROASTED TOMATOES WITH GARLIC AND LIME

ROOTS AND
tubers

Vegetables that grow underground—either the enlarged roots of plants or the tubers from which both plants and roots develop—make up an extensive group ranging from standbys such as potatoes and carrots to Jerusalem artichokes. Many of these vegetables share a pleasing sweet flavor.

Turnips and rutabagas (swedes) are related root vegetables. Rutabagas usually grow larger than turnips and have golden yellow flesh, whereas turnips are white. Parsnips, roots that resemble large carrots—and are, in fact, in the carrot family—have ivory-colored flesh. Sweet potatoes, though not related to their namesake, lend themselves to many of the same preparations as the popular potato.

Mature roots and tubers are generally peeled before cooking. Young vegetables, such as baby carrots and new potatoes, and Jerusalem artichokes can simply be washed and cooked in their skins.

When buying roots and tubers, select firm, unwrinkled specimens that are relatively heavy in proportion to their size. The green tops of turnips and beets can be eaten. Store roots and tubers, unwashed, with their leaves removed, in a cool, dark place for up to two weeks. Store leaves in the vegetable crisper of the refrigerator for up to one week.

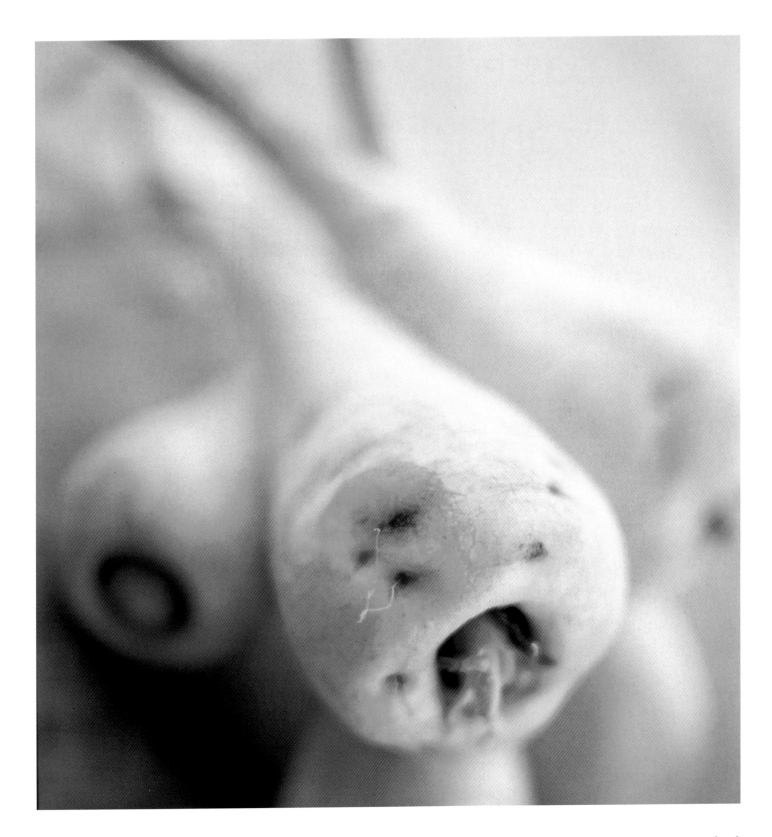

Roasted sweet potato and chili mash

4 medium sweet potatoes

1/3 cup (3 fl oz/90 ml) olive oil

sea salt and freshly ground black pepper to taste

3 teaspoons vegetable oil

1 small red chili pepper, seeded and chopped

2 cloves garlic, crushed

olive oil, for serving

Preheat oven to 400°F (200°C/Gas 6). Place whole, unpeeled sweet potatoes on a parchment-lined (baking paper–lined) baking sheet. Bake until potatoes are tender when pierced with a skewer, 30–40 minutes. Remove from oven and allow to stand until cool enough to handle, 5–10 minutes.

Peel sweet potatoes, place pulp in a bowl and mash until smooth. Gradually beat in olive oil, salt and pepper. Cover and keep warm.

Heat vegetable oil in a small pan over medium heat. Add chili pepper and garlic and cook until aromatic, about 1 minute. Remove from heat and add to potatoes. Mix well.

Serve hot, drizzled with extra olive oil if desired.

Serves 4–6 as an accompaniment

ROASTED SWEET POTATO AND CHILI MASH

Jerusalem artichokes with spicy vegetables

8 medium Jerusalem artichokes

2 tablespoons vegetable oil

1 onion, chopped

1 clove garlic, crushed

1 small red chili pepper, seeded and finely chopped

1/2 red bell pepper (capsicum), seeded and finely chopped

1 small green zucchini (courgette), chopped

1 medium tomato, chopped

2 oz (60 g) button mushrooms, sliced

sea salt and freshly ground black pepper to taste

1 tablespoon chopped fresh flat-leaf parsley, for garnish

Preheat oven to 350°F (180°C/Gas 4). Prick artichokes several times with a fork. Place on a parchment-lined (baking paper–lined) baking sheet. Bake until soft when pierced with a skewer, about 30 minutes. Time will depend on size of artichokes, as they vary greatly.

About 10 minutes before artichokes are ready, warm oil in a frying pan over medium heat. Add onion, garlic and chili pepper, and cook until onion softens, about 2 minutes. Add bell pepper, zucchini and tomato. Cover and cook over low heat, stirring occasionally, for about 5 minutes. Stir in mushrooms and cook until mushrooms soften, about 1 minute. Add salt and pepper to taste.

Remove artichokes from oven, place on a serving plate and slit open lengthwise.

Top each with 1 tablespoon spicy vegetable mixture, and garnish with chopped parsley. Serve remaining vegetable mixture in a bowl.

Serves 4

JERUSALEM ARTICHOKES WITH SPICY VEGETABLES 3 3

Roasted root vegetable medley

1 medium sweet potato

2 large carrots

1 medium parsnip

2 small turnips

2 small beets (beetroots)

3 medium potatoes

1 red bell pepper (capsicum), seeds removed

2 large green zucchini (courgettes)

1 large red (Spanish) onion, cut into 8 wedges

2 cloves garlic, slivered

$1/4$ cup (2 fl oz/60 ml) extra virgin olive oil

sea salt and freshly ground black pepper to taste

6 sprigs fresh rosemary

5 oz (150 g) preferred pasta

2 tablespoons butter

balsamic vinegar, for serving

Preheat oven to 400°F (200°C/Gas 6). Cut vegetables into uniform 2-inch (5-cm) cubes. There is no need to peel the vegetables. Place in a large oiled baking dish, then drizzle with oil. Sprinkle salt and pepper over vegetables and dot with rosemary sprigs. Bake until vegetables are tender, 25–30 minutes. Turn vegetables at least 3 times during cooking.

Cook pasta as directed on package, then drain, add butter and toss.

Serve roasted vegetables and pasta separately. Drizzle vegetables with balsamic vinegar to taste.

Serves 4

ROASTED ROOT VEGETABLE MEDLEY

Curried parsnip soup with parsnip chips

1/4 cup (2 fl oz/60 ml) vegetable oil

1 large onion, chopped

2 cloves garlic, crushed

1 teaspoon ground turmeric

1/2 teaspoon ground cumin

1/2 teaspoon ground ginger

1/2 small chili pepper, seeded and sliced

1 1/4 lb (625 g) parsnips, peeled and chopped

2 cooking apples, peeled, cored and chopped

4 cups (32 fl oz/1 L) vegetable stock

sea salt and freshly ground black pepper to taste

1 cup (8 fl oz/250 ml) cream

FOR PARSNIP CHIPS

4 parsnips, peeled

3 cups (24 fl oz/750 ml) vegetable oil, for
  deep-frying

Warm oil in a large saucepan over medium heat. Add onion and garlic and cook until onion softens, about 2 minutes. Stir in turmeric, cumin, ginger and chili pepper, and cook for 3 minutes, stirring occasionally. Add parsnips and apples and stir well. Cover and cook for 5 minutes, stirring occasionally. Stir in stock and season with salt and pepper. Bring mixture to a boil over high heat, then reduce heat, cover and simmer until parsnips are soft, 30–40 minutes.

To make parsnip chips: Thinly slice each parsnip lengthwise with a vegetable peeler. Heat oil in a large, deep, heavy-bottomed saucepan or deep-fat fryer until it reaches 375°F (190°C) on a deep-frying thermometer or until a small cube of bread dropped into oil sizzles and turns golden. Working in handfuls, add parsnip slices to hot oil and deep-fry until golden, about 1 minute. Using a slotted spoon, remove chips from oil and drain on paper towels.

Remove soup from heat and transfer to a large bowl. Working in batches, ladle into a food processor and process until smooth, about 20 seconds. Return soup to saucepan and heat through over medium heat, about 5 minutes. Stir in cream just before serving. Ladle into serving bowls and top with crisp parsnip chips.

Serves 6

Roasted potatoes with rosemary

12 medium potatoes, peeled

2 tablespoons olive oil

3 cloves garlic, crushed

2 tablespoons roughly chopped fresh rosemary

1 tablespoon sea salt

sea salt, for serving

Preheat oven to 400°F (200°C/Gas 6). Place potatoes on a parchment-lined (baking paper–lined) baking sheet.

Combine olive oil and garlic in a small bowl. Drizzle potatoes liberally with oil and garlic, then sprinkle evenly with rosemary leaves and salt. Bake, turning occasionally, until golden and crisp, 30–35 minutes.

Remove from oven and serve piping hot with extra salt.

Serves 4–6 as an accompaniment

ROASTED POTATOES WITH ROSEMARY

Baby beet salad with aioli

4 bunches baby beets (beetroots), red and golden
  if possible

FOR AIOLI
6 cloves garlic, crushed
3 egg yolks
pinch salt
1 teaspoon Dijon mustard
2 teaspoons lemon juice
1¼ cups (10 fl oz/300 ml) olive oil
white pepper to taste

TO SERVE
½ red (Spanish) onion, chopped
2 handfuls baby beet (beetroot) leaves
sea salt and freshly ground black pepper
olive oil, for drizzling

Cut off beet tops, leaving 2 inches (5 cm) of stem. Reserve leaves. Scrub beets with a soft brush. Bring a saucepan of water to a boil. Add beets, reduce heat, cover and simmer beets until tender, about 20 minutes. Remove from heat and allow beets to cool in liquid. When beets are cool enough to handle, slip off skins and trim stems. Refrigerate until ready to serve.

To make aioli: Place garlic, egg yolks, salt and mustard in a food processor and process until just combined, about 10 seconds. With the motor still running, add lemon juice, then add oil very slowly, in drops from a teaspoon. As mixture thickens, increase flow of oil, so it becomes a steady stream. Taste and add white pepper and a little more lemon juice if desired. (If mixture becomes too thick, add 1 tablespoon hot water just before serving.) Spoon aioli into 4 small bowls and refrigerate until ready to serve.

Arrange beet leaves on serving plates and top with cooked baby beets. Sprinkle beets with chopped onion and salt and pepper and drizzle liberally with olive oil. Serve with chilled aioli.

Serves 4–6

BABY BEET SALAD WITH AIOLI

Sweet potato and ricotta tart

1¹/₂ lb (750 g) soft ricotta cheese, well drained

1¹/₂ cups (6 oz/180 g) freshly grated parmesan cheese

5 eggs

2 cups (2 oz/60 g) arugula (rocket) leaves

¹/₃ cup (¹/₃ oz/10 g) fresh flat-leaf parsley leaves

1 tablespoon grated white onion

8 fresh sage leaves, stems removed

¹/₂ teaspoon sea salt

freshly ground black pepper to taste

1 medium sweet potato, peeled

1 tablespoon olive oil

olive oil, for serving

fresh sage leaves, for serving

sea salt, for serving

Preheat oven to 325°F (170°C/Gas 3). Place ricotta, parmesan and eggs in a food processor. Process until a smooth paste forms, about 20 seconds. Add arugula, parsley, onion, sage and salt and pepper to taste. Blend until smooth, about 30 seconds. Spoon cheese mixture into a well-oiled, 8-inch (20-cm), deep springform pan.

Thinly slice sweet potato lengthwise with a vegetable peeler. Arrange slices on top of tart. Drizzle with olive oil. Bake until cheese mixture is firm, about 1 hour. (Cover top of tart loosely with aluminum foil if it starts to brown too much during cooking.)

Remove tart from oven. Allow to cool to room temperature before removing from pan. Slice into wedges and serve drizzled with olive oil and sprinkled with sage leaves and salt.

Serves 5–6

Hint

Tart can be covered and refrigerated for up to 3 days.

SWEET POTATO AND RICOTTA TART

The bulb family includes onions, leeks and garlic, and the squash family comprises pumpkins, zucchinis (courgettes) and cucumbers. Squashes range in size from finger-length zucchini to huge pumpkins that are too heavy to hold in one hand. Their flesh has a fairly sweet flavor and a high water content.

Onions, leeks and garlic have been indispensable in cooking since the beginning of civilization. Over the centuries, countless onion varieties have been developed, from generally mild purple, red and white onions to the more pungent yellow (brown) varieties.

Scallions (shallots/spring onions), also known as green onions, are young onions that have been picked before the bulb has matured. Both the white bottom section and the tender green tops are used raw or cooked. Leeks, milder than onions and scallions, generally require a thorough rinsing before cooking to remove any dirt and grit. Garlic, when raw, is the most pungent of the whole family, although cooking subdues its sharpness.

Store onions and garlic in a cool, dark place for a few weeks, and scallions and leeks in a plastic bag in the vegetable crisper of the refrigerator for up to one week.

Squashes are categorized as summer or winter varieties. Summer squashes such as zucchini, crookneck and pattypan are picked when immature. Their skin and seeds are edible. The flowers are edible, prepared by deep-frying, sauteing or braising. Winter squashes, by contrast, are harvested when fully grown, and most types, including pumpkin, butternut and acorn, have tough skin, hard seeds and starchy flesh.

Store summer squashes in the vegetable crisper of the refrigerator for three or four days, and winter squashes in a cool, dark place for up to one month.

Oven-roasted onions with herb seasoning

6 medium yellow (brown) onions

1 tablespoon butter

1 clove garlic, crushed

4 oz (125 g) button mushrooms, chopped

1/2 cup (1 oz/30 g) fresh white breadcrumbs

2 tablespoons chopped fresh flat-leaf parsley

1 teaspoon chopped fresh thyme leaves

sea salt and freshly ground black pepper to taste

1/2 cup (4 fl oz/125 ml) vegetable stock

1/4 cup (2 fl oz/60 ml) dry white wine

1 tablespoon butter, chopped

Preheat oven to 350°F (180°C/Gas 4). Using a sharp knife, cut a thin slice from bottom of each onion, so that it stands steady. Using a teaspoon, scoop out inside of each onion, leaving a 1/4-inch (6-mm) shell. Finely chop scooped-out onion flesh. Reserve 2 tablespoons chopped onion and set aside. Save the remainder for another use.

Place onion shells in a large saucepan and cover with cold water. Bring water to a boil over medium heat, then remove from heat. Drain onions and place upside down on a wire rack.

Melt butter in a frying pan over medium heat. Add reserved chopped onion and garlic and cook until onion softens, about 2 minutes. Add mushrooms and stir gently until mushrooms soften, about 3 minutes. Remove from heat and add breadcrumbs, parsley, thyme and salt and pepper to taste. Allow mixture to cool slightly.

Spoon seasoning into onion shells, pressing it in firmly. Place onion shells in a lightly oiled baking dish just large enough to hold them. Combine stock and wine in a measuring cup and pour around onions. Top with chopped butter. Bake until onions are tender, 35–40 minutes.

Remove from oven and serve hot.

Serves 6 as an accompaniment

Creamy leek purée

2 lb (1 kg) leeks

1 green apple, peeled, cored and chopped

2 cups (16 fl oz/500 ml) vegetable stock

1 tablespoon peeled and grated fresh ginger

2 tablespoons butter

2 tablespoons cream

1 teaspoon sea salt, or to taste

freshly ground black pepper to taste

Trim leeks, and discard root end and green tops. Cut remaining sections in half lengthwise, then wash thoroughly and roughly chop into 1-inch (2.5-cm) pieces. Place leeks in a deep saucepan. Add apple, stock and ginger. Bring to a boil over medium heat. Reduce heat, cover and simmer until leeks are tender, 10–15 minutes. Remove from heat and allow to cool slightly.

Pour mixture in a large bowl. Working in batches, ladle into a food processor and process until it forms a smooth purée, about 20 seconds. Transfer purée to a smaller saucepan. Place over medium heat, add butter and stir until butter melts, about 2 minutes. Stir in cream, salt and pepper to taste. Continue stirring over low heat until heated through, about 1 minute.

Remove from heat and serve warm.

Serves 4–6 as an accompaniment

CREAMY LEEK PURÉE

Baked squash with tomato and basil risotto

FOR SQUASH

4 golden nugget squashes (substitute acorn,
   dumpling, or Danish squash)

3 tablespoons olive oil

6 cloves garlic, crushed

FOR RISOTTO

5 cups (40 fl oz/1.25 L) vegetable stock

1/2 cup (4 fl oz/125 ml) dry white wine

3 tablespoons olive oil

1 onion, chopped

1 1/8 cup (8 oz/250 g) arborio rice

2 medium tomatoes, seeds removed and chopped
   (see page 11 for step-by-step instructions)

1/2 cup (2 oz/60 g) freshly grated parmesan cheese

1 tablespoon butter

1/4 cup (3/4 oz/25 g) chopped fresh basil

sea salt and freshly ground black pepper to taste

1/2 cup (2 oz/60 g) freshly grated parmesan, for
   serving

Preheat oven to 350°F (180°C/Gas 4). To prepare golden nugget squashes: Using a strong, sharp knife, cut each squash in half through stem. Scoop out and discard seeds. Trim bottom of each squash half so it sits firmly. Combine oil and garlic in a small bowl, then brush on cut surfaces. Place halves, cut side up, in an oiled baking dish. Pour 1/2 cup (4 fl oz/125 ml) hot water around squashes. Cover with aluminum foil and bake for 30 minutes.

Meanwhile, to make risotto: Place stock and wine in a saucepan and bring to a boil over high heat. Reduce heat until liquid is just simmering. Keep liquid simmering.

Warm oil in a medium to large saucepan over medium heat. Add onion and cook until it softens, about 2 minutes. Add rice and cook, stirring constantly, until rice is coated with oil, about 1 minute. Add 1 cup (8 fl oz/250 ml) liquid to rice, stirring constantly. Reduce heat and allow risotto to simmer gently, continuing to stir. As rice takes up liquid, gradually add remaining liquid, 1 cup (8 fl oz/250 ml) at a time, until all is absorbed by rice, and rice is al dente and creamy, about 25 minutes. Stir in tomatoes, then cover and cook over low heat for 5 minutes. Remove from heat and stir in parmesan, butter and basil. Season with salt and pepper.

Remove squash halves from oven and pat centers dry with paper towels. Reduce oven temperature to 225°F (110°C/Gas 1/4). Spoon risotto into each half. Place halves in oven for 10 minutes before serving.

Arrange on serving plates and accompany with extra grated parmesan.

Serves 4–6

BAKED SQUASH WITH TOMATO AND BASIL RISOTTO

Cheese and zucchini fritters

3 oz (90 g) goat cheese

1 teaspoon chopped fresh thyme

2 teaspoons chopped fresh chervil

2 teaspoons chopped fresh flat-leaf parsley

3/4 cup (4 oz/125 g) all-purpose (plain) flour

pinch sea salt

1 egg

1 tablespoon olive oil

1/3 cup (3 fl oz/90 ml) beer

12 small zucchini (courgette) flowers

3 cups (24 fl oz/750 ml) vegetable oil, for
  deep-frying

sea salt, for serving

arugula (rocket) leaves, for serving

Preheat oven to 225°F (110°C/Gas ¼). Place cheese, thyme, chervil and parsley in a bowl. Using a fork, blend together well.

Place flour and salt in a food processor. Add egg, oil and beer. Process until smooth, about 20 seconds. Transfer batter to a bowl. Cover and allow to stand for 10 minutes.

Meanwhile, clean zucchini flowers. You may need to trim flowers to 1 inch (2.5 cm) if they are too long. (Flowers will break away from sections during cooking if they are too heavy.) Carefully open each flower and insert 1–2 teaspoons of cheese mixture, depending on size of flower. Gently press petals closed.

Heat oil in a large, deep, heavy-bottomed saucepan or deep-fat fryer until it reaches 375°F (190°C) on a deep-frying thermometer or until a small cube of bread dropped into the oil sizzles and turns golden.

Working in batches, dip flowers into batter. If batter is a little thick, blend in 1 tablespoon milk. Deep-fry flowers in hot oil until golden and crisp, about 1 minute. Drain on paper towels. Keep warm in oven.

Serve immediately with salt. Serve arugula leaves separately.

Serves 4

CHEESE AND ZUCCHINI FRITTERS

Watermelon with red onion salsa

12 wedges chilled watermelon, about $^3/_8$ inch
   (12 mm) thick

1 red (Spanish) onion, chopped

3 oz (90 g) feta cheese, cut into $^1/_2$-inch (12-mm)
   cubes

3 tablespoons olive oil

freshly ground black pepper to taste

olive oil, for serving

freshly ground black pepper, for serving

Place 2 watermelon wedges on each serving plate. In a bowl, combine onion, feta, oil and plenty of black pepper. Spoon over watermelon. Serve chilled, drizzled with olive oil and sprinkled with freshly ground black pepper.

Serves 6

Chilled cucumber and ginger soup

12 small English (hothouse) cucumbers, peeled and
   seeded

3 teaspoons sea salt

2 teaspoons peeled and grated fresh ginger

freshly ground black pepper to taste

$^3/_4$ cup (6 oz/180 g) plain (natural) yogurt

1 small English (hothouse) cucumber, peeled,
   seeded and sliced, for garnish

dill sprigs, for garnish

Slice cucumbers in half lengthwise. Sprinkle with 2 tablespoons salt, place in a colander and allow to stand for 30 minutes. Rinse cucumbers well under cold water. Roughly chop and place in a food processor. Add ginger, remaining salt and pepper. Process until mixture forms a thick purée, about 20 seconds.

Transfer 1 cup (8 oz/250 g) purée to a bowl. Cover and refrigerate. Firmly press remaining purée through a fine sieve to produce a clear cucumber-flavored liquid. Discard solids. Cover and refrigerate cucumber liquid. The purée and liquid should be left in refrigerator for 1 hour.

Place ¼ cup (2 oz/60 g) cucumber purée in center of each serving bowl. Pour cucumber liquid around pulp. Top each serving with 2 tablespoons yogurt. Garnish with cucumber slices and dill sprigs.

Serves 3 or 4

CHILLED CUCUMBER AND GINGER SOUP

Pumpkin and zucchini curry

4 cloves garlic, peeled

1-inch (2.5-cm) piece fresh ginger, peeled

1 red (Spanish) onion, roughly chopped

1 teaspoon ground cumin

1 teaspoon ground coriander

1/2 teaspoon ground cloves

1 teaspoon ground fennel seeds

2 teaspoons Asian sesame oil

2 tablespoons vegetable oil

1 or 2 small red chili peppers (to taste), seeded
   and finely chopped

2 1/2 cups (20 fl oz/625 ml) thick coconut cream

3 kaffir lime leaves

1 lb (500 g) pumpkin flesh, cut into 1-inch
   (2.5-cm) cubes

4 zucchini (courgettes), cut into 1-inch (2.5-cm)
   cubes

2 teaspoons fish sauce

2 1/2 cups (2 1/2 oz/75 g) loosely packed baby
   spinach leaves

steamed jasmine rice, for serving

Place garlic, ginger, onion, cumin, coriander, cloves, fennel seeds and sesame oil in a small food processor. Process until mixture forms a smooth paste, about 20 seconds.

Warm vegetable oil in a wok or large saucepan over medium heat. Add spice paste and chili peppers and stir-fry until aromatic, 1–2 minutes. Stir in coconut cream, kaffir lime leaves and pumpkin. Cook at a steady simmer over medium–low heat for 10 minutes. Add zucchini and fish sauce and simmer until vegetables are tender, about 10 minutes. Remove curry from heat and gently stir in spinach.

Serve hot with steamed jasmine rice.

Serves 4–6

Hint

If you don't have a small processor, use a regular-sized processor or mortar and pestle.

PUMPKIN AND ZUCCHINI CURRY

The best-known edible pod is the green bean, or snap bean. The most common variety is green. There is also a purple bean that turns green when cooked, and a waxy yellow variety. The French haricot vert, also green, is very slender and, when cooked, is tender and sweet. Runner beans and long, or snake, beans, used in Asian cooking, are available fresh most of the year.

Other types of beans are cultivated for their seeds. Most are available dried, but some seasonal varieties, such as fava (broad) beans and cranberry beans, are also sold fresh.

Of the members of the pea family, one variety eaten in its entirety is the snow pea (mange-tout). Used in Asian stir-fry dishes, snow peas are best when their crisp texture is retained during cooking.

Store fresh peas and beans in the vegetable crisper of the refrigerator for several days and do not shell until ready to use. Store dried beans in an airtight container in a cool, dry place for six months.

The seeds, or kernels, of sweet corn are sweetest when prepared soon after removal from the cob. Yellow and white varieties are found in well-stocked supermarkets. Look for corn that is still in its husk. Before purchase, peel back the husk slightly to make sure the kernels are plump and smooth, not dry and wrinkled. Though corn is best prepared the same day it is bought, if you must store it, wrap in damp paper towels and keep in the coldest part of the refrigerator. Do not remove the husk until just before cooking.

Pea, leek and asparagus risotto

8 oz (250 g) asparagus

6 cups (48 fl oz/1.5 L) vegetable stock

3 tablespoons olive oil

1 medium leek, trimmed, washed and finely sliced

2 cloves garlic, crushed

12 oz (375 g) fresh peas

$1^1/_4$ cup ($8^3/_4$ oz/275 g) arborio rice

$3^1/_2$ oz (105 g) freshly grated parmesan cheese

1 tablespoon butter

$^1/_4$ cup ($^1/_2$ oz/15 g) freshly chopped flat-leaf
   parsley

sea salt and freshly ground black pepper to taste

Trim asparagus and cut each stalk crosswise into 4 pieces. Bring a saucepan of water to a boil. Add asparagus and cook for 1 minute, then remove pan from heat, drain asparagus, and refresh in cold water. Drain again and set aside.

Place stock in a saucepan and bring to a boil over high heat. Reduce heat until stock is just simmering.

Warm oil in a medium to large saucepan over medium heat. Add leek and garlic and cook until leek softens, about 1 minute. Stir in peas and ½ cup (4 fl oz/125 ml) stock. Cook for 1 minute, stirring constantly. Add rice and cook, stirring constantly, for 2 minutes. Add 1 cup (8 fl oz/250 ml) stock, stirring constantly. Reduce heat and allow risotto to simmer gently, continuing to stir. As rice takes up liquid, gradually add remaining stock, 1 cup (8 fl oz/250 ml) at a time, until all is absorbed by rice, and rice is al dente and creamy, about 25 minutes. Stir in asparagus, parmesan, butter and parsley.

Season with salt and pepper and serve immediately.

Serves 4–6

PEA, LEEK AND ASPARAGUS RISOTTO

Sweet corn fritters

1 lb (500 g) potatoes, peeled and cubed

1 egg, beaten

$^1/_4$ cup (2 fl oz/60 ml) cream

$^1/_4$ cup (1$^1/_2$ oz/45 g) all-purpose (plain) flour

kernels from 2 corn cobs, about 2 cups

   (12 oz/375 g) (see page 10 for step-by-step

   instructions)

$^1/_4$ cup ($^1/_4$ oz/7 g) cilantro (coriander) leaves,

   finely chopped

1 egg white

sea salt and freshly ground black pepper to taste

3 tablespoons vegetable oil

$^1/_3$ cup (3 fl oz/90 ml) Thai sweet chili sauce,

   for dipping

Preheat oven to 225°F (110°C/Gas ¼). Bring a saucepan of salted water to a boil. Add potatoes and cook until soft but not mushy, 6–8 minutes. Drain well, place in a bowl and mash with a fork or potato masher. Allow to cool slightly. Add egg and cream and mix well. Stir in flour, corn and cilantro.

In a bowl, using a balloon whisk or electric beater, beat egg white until soft peaks form. Gently fold egg white into corn mixture and season with salt and pepper.

Warm oil in a heavy-bottomed frying pan over medium heat. For each fritter, spoon 2 tablespoons corn mixture into hot pan. Cook fritters until golden, 2–3 minutes per side. Remove from pan and drain on paper towels. Keep warm in oven.

Serve with Thai sweet chili sauce for dipping.

Serves 4–6

SWEET CORN FRITTERS

Stir-fried fennel, celery, snow peas and bean sprouts

2 cloves garlic, roughly chopped

$^1/_2$ cup ($^1/_2$ oz/15 g) cilantro (coriander) leaves

1 stalk lemongrass, bottom 3 inches (7.5 cm) only, inner stalks roughly chopped

juice of 1 lime

2 tablespoons soy sauce

2 tablespoons superfine (caster) sugar

sea salt and freshly ground black pepper to taste

2 tablespoons vegetable oil

1-inch (2.5-cm) piece fresh ginger, peeled and finely chopped

1 green chili pepper, seeded and thinly sliced

12 scallions (shallots/spring onions), roots trimmed, sliced

2 bulbs fennel, roots and leaves trimmed and thinly sliced

2 celery stalks, sliced

$3^1/_2$ oz (105 g) snow peas (mange-tout)

$^2/_3$ cup (5 fl oz/150 ml) thick coconut cream

$3^1/_2$ oz (105 g) bean sprouts, rinsed

$^1/_4$ cup ($1^1/_2$ oz/45 g) unsalted roasted peanuts

steamed jasmine rice, for serving

Place garlic, cilantro, lemongrass and lime juice in a mortar and using a pestle, pound into a smooth paste. Alternatively, place in a small food processor and process to form a smooth paste, about 20 seconds. Transfer to a bowl and add soy sauce, sugar, and salt and pepper to taste.

Warm oil in a wok or large frying pan over medium heat. Add ginger, chili pepper and scallions, and stir-fry until aromatic, about 2 minutes. Add fennel, celery and snow peas, and stir-fry for 3 minutes. Add spice paste and coconut cream and cook, continuing to stir, until sauce thickens slightly, about 2 minutes. Stir in bean sprouts. Remove from heat.

Sprinkle with peanuts and serve immediately with steamed jasmine rice.

Serves 4

STIR-FRIED FENNEL. CELERY. SNOW PEAS AND SPROUTS

Mixed bean and feta salad

1 lb (500 g) fresh beans, preferably a combination
   of green and yellow lima (butter) beans

1 teaspoon grainy mustard

2 tablespoons balsamic vinegar

5 tablespoons extra virgin olive oil

freshly ground black pepper to taste

4 oz (125 g) feta cheese, crumbled

1/3 cup (1/2 oz/15 g) small fresh basil leaves

Bring a saucepan of salted water to a boil. Add beans and cook until just tender–crisp, 2–3 minutes. Drain and refresh in a bowl of ice water. Drain again, then pat beans dry with paper towels. Place beans in a bowl, cover and refrigerate until ready to serve.

Place mustard, vinegar, olive oil and plenty of pepper in a screw-top jar and shake until well combined.

Pour dressing over beans and toss until beans are thoroughly coated.

Arrange beans on a serving plate and top with feta and basil leaves.

Serves 4

MIXED BEAN AND FETA SALAD

Pea and lettuce soup

2 lb (1 kg) peas in their pods

2 tablespoons vegetable oil

2 medium leeks, trimmed, washed and cut into
   $^1/_2$-inch (12-mm) pieces

2 large potatoes, peeled and cut into $^1/_2$-inch
   (12-mm) cubes

1/2 teaspoon sugar

4 cups (32 fl oz/1 L) vegetable stock

sea salt and freshly ground black pepper to taste

1 head iceberg (web) lettuce, trimmed and
   chopped

$^1/_3$ cup (3 fl oz/90 ml) crème fraîche

1 tablespoon chopped chives, for garnish

Remove peas from pods and discard pods. Warm oil in a large saucepan over medium heat. Add leeks and potatoes and cook for 2 minutes, stirring constantly. Add peas, sugar and stock. Increase heat to bring mixture to a boil, then reduce heat to medium–low until liquid is at a steady simmer. Cover and simmer for 10 minutes.

Stir in lettuce, cover and cook until potatoes are tender, about 3 minutes.

Pour soup into a large bowl. Working in batches, ladle soup into a food processor and process until smooth, about 30 seconds. Return soup to saucepan and stir over low heat until heated through, about 3 minutes.

Serve in heated bowls, topping each serving with crème fraîche and chives.

Serves 4–6

PEA AND LETTUCE SOUP

The list of vegetables in this category is long and diverse. Leaf vegetables include spinach, lettuces—from lettuces that form compact heads to looseleaf types such as red leaf—and the many Chinese varieties found increasingly in supermarkets. Their tastes range from the peppery bite of arugula (rocket) to the sweetness of young spinach.

Leaf vegetables are best consumed as soon as possible after harvesting. Select unblemished specimens with good color and store, unwashed, in a plastic bag in the vegetable crisper of the refrigerator for up to four days.

Flower vegetables include cabbage and some of its relatives: cauliflower, broccoli and brussels sprouts. Among the many types of cabbage are compact heads with red leaves and long heads with crinkled green leaves. Brussels sprouts resemble miniature heads of green cabbage.

Store cabbage and their relatives in the vegetable crisper of the refrigerator for up to one week.

Mesclun salad with pesto avocado

FOR PESTO

$^1/_2$ cup ($^3/_4$ oz/25 g) well packed basil leaves

$^1/_2$ cup ($^3/_4$ oz/25 g) well packed chopped arugula (rocket) leaves

2 oz (60 g) pine nuts, toasted

2 cloves garlic, chopped

pinch sea salt

juice of 1 lemon

2 oz (60 g) freshly grated parmesan cheese

$^1/_2$ cup (4 fl oz/125 ml) extra virgin olive oil

FOR SALAD

2 ripe avocados

juice of 1 lemon

2 tablespoons balsamic vinegar

2 tablespoons extra virgin olive oil

4 cups (2$^1/_2$ oz/75 g) loosely packed mixed salad leaves (mesclun)

To make pesto: Place basil, arugula, pine nuts, garlic, salt, lemon juice and parmesan in a food processor. Process until well blended, about 15 seconds. With food processor running, gradually add the oil. Process until mixture has consistency of thick paste. Use a little less or a little more oil if necessary, to achieve right consistency. Spoon pesto into a screw-top jar and refrigerate until ready to use.

To make salad: Slice each avocado in half through stem, and remove pit and skin. Cut into 1-inch (2.5-cm) cubes and place in a bowl. Add lemon juice and gently toss avocados in juice. Add 3 tablespoons pesto to bowl and gently toss avocados until coated. (Store remaining pesto in refrigerator, and use for salads, pasta, sandwiches and sauces.)

In a small bowl, combine balsamic vinegar and olive oil.

Place salad leaves in a serving bowl and drizzle with vinegar and oil. Add pesto avocado, toss and serve immediately.

Serves 4 as a side dish

MESCLUN SALAD WITH PESTO AVOCADO

Asian greens with lemon and ginger oil

⅓ cup (3 fl oz/90 ml) sunflower oil

finely grated zest (rind) of 2 lemons

1 lemongrass stalk, bottom 3 inches (7.5 cm) only,
   inner stalks roughly chopped

3 teaspoons peeled and grated fresh ginger

1 lb (500 g) mixed Asian greens, such as bok choy,
   choy sum and Chinese cabbage

pinch sea salt

pinch sugar

juice of 1 lemon

lemon wedges, for serving

Place oil, lemon zest, lemongrass and ginger in a screw-top jar and shake until well combined. Set aside in a warm place for 5 days so flavors infuse oil. After 5 days, strain oil and discard solids. Seal and store lemon and ginger oil in a cool, dark place.

Wash greens well. Pat dry with paper towels. Trim roots from greens and cut into 2-inch (5-cm) lengths. If using bok choy, remove dark outer leaves, separate younger leaves and trim ends.

Warm 2 tablespoons lemon and ginger oil in a wok or frying pan over medium heat. Add greens and stir-fry until tender-crisp, 3–4 minutes. Remove from heat and stir in salt, sugar and lemon juice. Serve immediately, accompanied with lemon wedges.

Serves 4

ASIAN GREENS WITH LEMON AND GINGER OIL

Cauliflower coconut soup

2 tablespoons vegetable oil

1 clove garlic, crushed

1 medium leek, trimmed, washed and sliced

1 lb (500 g) cauliflower florets

2 stalks celery, sliced

1 tablespoon Thai red curry paste

2½ cups (20 fl oz/625 ml) vegetable stock

1 cup (8 fl oz/250 ml) thick coconut cream

10 oz (300 g) can lima (butter) or cannellini
  beans, drained

sea salt and freshly ground black pepper to taste

celery leaves, for garnish

¼ cup (¼ oz/7 g) whole cilantro (coriander)
  leaves, for garnish

Warm oil in a large saucepan over medium heat. When oil is hot but not smoking, add garlic, leek, cauliflower and celery and cook, stirring, over medium heat, for 5 minutes. Stir in curry paste and vegetable stock and cook, increasing heat if necessary, until mixture is at a steady simmer. Cover and allow to simmer until cauliflower is tender, about 10 minutes.

Add coconut cream, beans, and salt and pepper to taste. Heat soup through, about 3 minutes. Do not allow soup to boil.

Ladle into serving bowls and garnish with celery and cilantro leaves.

Serves 4

CAULIFLOWER COCONUT SOUP

Lettuce, carrot and feta salad

4 medium carrots, peeled

1 head baby romaine (cos) lettuce or $^1/_2$ head normal-sized romaine (cos) lettuce

4 oz (125 g) firm feta cheese, cut into $^1/_2$-inch (12-mm) cubes

$^1/_4$ cup (3/4 oz/7 g) fresh dill, chopped

3 tablespoons lemon juice

2 tablespoons olive oil

$^1/_4$ teaspoon sea salt

freshly ground black pepper to taste

Cut carrots in half lengthwise. Using a vegetable peeler, slice carrots into thin long strips. Place strips in a bowl of ice water and place in refrigerator until carrot curls, about 15 minutes. Drain carrots and pat dry with paper towels.

Slice lettuce into 1-inch (2.5-cm) shreds. Combine carrots, lettuce, feta and dill in a serving bowl.

Combine lemon juice, olive oil and salt and pepper in a screw-top jar and shake well to mix. Pour dressing over salad and toss until well combined.

Serve chilled.

Serves 4 as a side dish

LETTUCE. CARROT AND FETA SALAD

Asian greens stir-fry with shiitake mushrooms

1 lb (500 g) Asian greens, such as bok choy, choy
    sum or Chinese cabbage

2 tablespoons vegetable oil

1 red bell pepper (capsicum), seeded and sliced
    into strips

1 small red chili pepper, seeded and sliced

10 scallions (shallots/spring onions), trimmed and
    sliced

2 celery stalks, sliced

1 lemongrass stalk, trimmed and chopped

2 cloves garlic, crushed

1 inch (2.5 cm) piece fresh ginger, peeled and
    chopped

6 oz (180 g) shiitake mushrooms, sliced

3 tablespoons soy sauce

cooked egg noodles or jasmine rice, for serving

Wash Asian greens well and pat dry with paper towels. Trim off root ends and slice greens into 2½-inch (6-cm) lengths.

Warm oil in a wok or large frying pan over medium heat, until oil is hot but not smoking. Add bell pepper, chili pepper, scallions, celery, lemongrass, garlic and ginger. Raise heat to medium-high and stir-fry for 2 minutes. Add greens and mushrooms and stir-fry for 2 minutes. Reduce heat to low, cover and allow mixture to cook slowly until greens are tender–crisp, about 2 minutes. Remove from heat and stir in soy sauce.

Serve immediately with egg noodles or jasmine rice.

Serves 4

ASIAN GREENS STIR-FRY WITH SHIITAKE MUSHROOMS   8 3

Chili broccoli with noodles

12 oz (375 g) egg noodles

1 1/2 lb (750 g) broccoli, cut into florets

3 tablespoons olive oil

1 medium red (Spanish) onion, chopped

2 cloves garlic, crushed

1 small red chili pepper, seeded and thinly sliced

sea salt and freshly ground black pepper to taste

balsamic vinegar, for drizzling

1/3 cup (1 1/2 oz/45 g) parmesan shavings, for
  serving

Cook noodles as directed on package, then drain and rinse. Meanwhile, bring a saucepan of water to a boil. Add broccoli florets and cook for 2 minutes. Drain and refresh in cold water. Drain again and set aside.

Warm oil in a wok or large frying pan. Add onion, garlic and chili pepper and stir-fry until onion softens, about 2 minutes. Stir in broccoli and cooked noodles. Stir-fry until heated through, about 3 minutes. Season with salt and pepper to taste.

Serve hot, drizzled with balsamic vinegar and topped with parmesan shavings.

Serves 4

Hint

To make parmesan shavings, use a vegetable peeler and shave thin curls from a block of fresh parmesan.

CHILI BROCCOLI WITH NOODLES

Brussels sprouts with peanut sauce

1 lb (500 g) brussels sprouts

2 tablespoons peanut butter

4 tablespoons soy sauce

2–3 tablespoons boiling water

Trim bottom of each brussels sprout, removing any dark outer leaves. Bring a saucepan of water to a boil. Add brussels sprouts, cover and cook until tender, 5–10 minutes. Drain, then cut brussels sprouts in half.

In a small bowl, combine peanut butter, soy sauce and boiling water.

Thread brussels sprout halves onto bamboo skewers and serve warm with peanut sauce.

Serves 4 as an accompaniment

BRUSSELS SPROUTS WITH PEANUT SAUCE

mushrooms

At one time, cooks were limited to the cultivated white mushrooms sold in most stores. Now, the varieties once used only by those who found them in specialty markets or had the skill to find them in the wild are cultivated and available in many supermarkets. Joining the common button are such varieties as morel, chanterelle, oyster, shiitake and enoki.

Mushrooms have meaty texture and absorb the flavors of the other ingredients in a recipe. Another plus is that they require little preparation. Just wipe the caps clean with a damp paper towel or remove any dirt with a mushroom brush.

Store fresh mushrooms in a paper bag in the refrigerator for up to seven days. Never place mushrooms in a plastic bag, which causes them to turn soggy.

Herb-filled mushrooms

6 medium mushrooms

1 tablespoon olive oil

3 cloves garlic, crushed

$^1/_2$ red (Spanish) onion, chopped

2 tablespoons chopped fresh flat-leaf parsley

$1^1/_2$ tablespoons chopped fresh marjoram

$1^1/_2$ tablespoons chopped fresh thyme

$^1/_2$ cup (1 oz/30 g) fresh white breadcrumbs

$^1/_4$ cup (1 oz/30 g) freshly grated parmesan cheese

sea salt and freshly ground black pepper to taste

3 teaspoons olive oil, for drizzling

thyme leaves, for garnish

Preheat oven to 400°F (200°C/Gas 6). Wipe mushrooms clean using a damp paper towel. Remove stems. Chop stems finely and set aside.

Warm oil in a frying pan over medium heat. Add garlic and onion and cook until onion softens, about 2 minutes. Stir in chopped mushroom stems and cook until they soften, 3–4 minutes.

Remove from heat and add parsley, marjoram, thyme, breadcrumbs, parmesan and salt and pepper to taste. Mix well. Divide mixture among mushroom caps, packing it well.

Place filled mushrooms, filled side up, on a parchment-lined (baking paper–lined) baking sheet. Drizzle with extra olive oil. Bake until golden, 15–20 minutes.

Serve hot, garnished with fresh thyme.

Serves 3 or 4

HERB-FILLED MUSHROOMS

Mixed mushrooms
on grilled Turkish bread

1 lb (500 g) mixed mushrooms, such as button,
  field, shiitake, oyster and cepes

2 tablespoons vegetable oil

2 tablespoons butter

2 cloves garlic, crushed

1 tablespoon balsamic vinegar

2 tablespoons chopped fresh flat-leaf parsley

2 teaspoons chopped fresh thyme

sea salt and freshly ground black pepper to taste

8 wedges Turkish bread

2 tablespoons olive oil

flat-leaf parsley, for garnish

Wipe mushrooms clean using a damp paper towel. Cut into even slices. Warm oil and butter in a heavy-bottomed frying pan over medium heat. Add garlic and fry until aromatic, about 1 minute. Stir in mushrooms and cook for 5 minutes, stirring constantly.

Remove from heat and add balsamic vinegar, parsley, thyme and salt and pepper to taste.

Preheat a broiler (grill) or barbecue. Brush both sides of bread with olive oil. Broil (grill) until golden, 1–2 minutes per side. Arrange grilled bread on serving plates and top with mushrooms. Serve garnished with parsley.

Serves 4

Hint

If Turkish bread is unavailable, use preferred, thickly sliced bread.

MIXED MUSHROOMS ON GRILLED TURKISH BREAD

Mini mushroom tarts

3 sheets pre-rolled frozen puff pastry

2 tablespoons butter

1 lb (500 g) button mushrooms, thinly sliced

3 sprigs thyme, stems removed

1 tablespoon cornstarch (cornflour)

$^1/_2$ cup (4 fl oz/125 ml) cream

sea salt and freshly ground black pepper to taste

12 tiny sprigs thyme, for garnish

Preheat oven to 375°F (190°C/Gas 5). Grease 2 jumbo muffin pans, each with a 6-muffins capacity.

Cut each sheet of pastry into quarters; each quarter will make 1 tart. Place pastry square in each muffin cup, leaving edges untrimmed. Cover each pastry square, with parchment (baking) paper, then add ¼ cup (2 oz/60 g) lentils, rice or baking weights, to weight paper and pastry. Bake until golden, about 12 minutes. Remove weights and paper, and place muffin pans back in oven for 5 minutes to dry out bottoms.

Melt butter in a large frying pan over medium heat. Add mushrooms and cook for 7 minutes. Stir in thyme leaves.

In a bowl, combine cornstarch and cream. Add to frying pan. Increase heat slightly and stir until sauce has thickened and heated through. Season with salt and pepper.

Fill tart shells with mushroom mixture and serve immediately, garnishing each with a thyme sprig.

Serves 4

MINI MUSHROOM TARTS

Within this section is one of the aristocrats of the vegetable domain—the asparagus—along with globe artichokes, fennel, celery and Belgian endive.

Asparagus is best enjoyed when it is in season and plentiful at the market. The most common variety is green. Spears of white asparagus, sold in some markets, are harvested before they grow aboveground. Asparagus is very perishable and should be stored, unwashed, in the vegetable crisper of the refrigerator for no more than three days.

The globe artichoke is the bud of a plant in the thistle family. Like asparagus, it is at its best when in season. Select heavy, compact, plump globes and avoid those with opened or curled leaves. Artichokes can be stored, unwashed, in the vegetable crisper of the refrigerator for several days.

Fennel and celery can be interchanged in some recipes, though their flavors differ noticeably. Fennel has hints of licorice and is somewhat sweeter than celery. In many recipes, there is no substitute for the fennel bulb and its sweet, aromatic taste.

Belgian endive (chicory/witloof) has a slightly bitter flavor and a crisp texture. Heads of endive may be cooked. Endive is also enjoyed raw, whether sliced or as separate leaves. Avoid buying heads with brownish leaves. Store endive in the vegetable crisper of the refrigerator for no more than four days.

STALKS AND SHOOTS

Baked baby fennel with parmesan

4 baby fennel bulbs

2 tablespoons butter, chopped

$^{1}/_{2}$ cup (2 oz/60 g) freshly grated parmesan cheese

1 teaspoon ground nutmeg

freshly ground black pepper to taste

Preheat oven to 350°F (180°C/Gas 4). Discard any bruised leaves from fennel bulbs and remove feathery fronds. Cut bulbs in half lengthwise. Bring a saucepan of water to a boil. Add fennel and cook until tender, 5–7 minutes. Do not overcook fennel or it will turn a dull gray and become very soft. Drain and refresh fennel under cold running water, then pat dry with paper towels.

Place fennel in a lightly oiled, shallow heatproof dish. Dot with butter and sprinkle with cheese, nutmeg and pepper to taste. Bake for 10 minutes.

Remove from oven, place under a hot broiler (grill) and cook until cheese melts, about 2 minutes. Serve hot.

Serves 4 as an accompaniment or entrée

BAKED BABY FENNEL WITH PARMESAN

Baked artichokes

6 globe artichokes (see page 9 for step-by-step
   instructions)
juice of 2 lemons
5 cloves garlic, crushed
1 onion, chopped
$^1/_4$ cup ($^1/_3$ oz/10 g) chopped fresh mint
$^1/_4$ cup ($^1/_3$ oz/10 g) chopped fresh flat-leaf parsley
$^1/_4$ cup ($^1/_3$ oz/10 g) chopped fresh rosemary
sea salt and freshly ground black pepper to taste
2 tablespoons extra virgin olive oil

Preheat oven to 350°F (180°C/Gas 4).
Hold each artichoke firmly and bend
stem until it snaps from bottom.
Remove outer leaves by pulling away
from artichoke and then downward to
break tough upper part from fleshy base.
Continue until you reach tender inner
leaves, which are yellowish green in color.

Using a stainless steel knife, cut off
one-third of artichoke top. Rub cut
surface with lemon juice (using about
half the juice) to prevent discoloration.
Remove prickly choke with a teaspoon.
Place artichokes in a bowl of water to which remaining lemon
juice has been added.

Combine garlic, onion, mint, parsley, rosemary and salt and
pepper to taste in a bowl.

Drain artichokes and pat dry with paper towels, then place in
an oiled baking dish just large enough to hold them. Stuff center
of each artichoke with herb mixture. Pour boiling water into pan
to reach about 1 inch (2.5 cm) up sides. Drizzle artichokes with
olive oil and bake until tender, 35–45 minutes.

Serve hot or cold.

Serves 6 as an accompaniment or entrée

BAKED ARTICHOKES

Grilled endive with goat cheese and walnuts

4 heads Belgian endive (witloof)

2 tablespoons extra virgin olive oil, for brushing

$^1/_2$ cup (4 fl oz/125 ml) extra virgin olive oil

6 tablespoons (3 fl oz/90 ml) balsamic vinegar

sea salt and freshly ground black pepper to taste

2 oz (60 g) goat cheese, crumbled

$^1/_4$ cup (1 oz/30 g) chopped walnuts

Preheat a broiler (grill). Cut each endive in half lengthwise and brush well with oil. Place endives, cut side down, on broiler pan and cook until lightly golden, about 2 minutes. Do not turn. Arrange endives on serving plates.

Combine olive oil, vinegar and salt and pepper to taste in a screw-top jar and shake well.

Drizzle over endives and top with goat cheese and walnuts.

Serves 4

GRILLED ENDIVE WITH GOAT CHEESE AND WALNUTS 103

Asparagus poached in red wine with cilantro

1/2 cup (4 fl oz/125 ml) olive oil

1/2 cup (4 fl oz/125 ml) red wine

2 tablespoons balsamic vinegar

1 teaspoon sugar

1 tablespoon coriander seeds, cracked

1 teaspoon cracked black pepper

13 oz (400 g) asparagus, stalks trimmed (see page
   12 for step-by-step instructions)

8 wedges Turkish bread, or any preferred, thickly
   sliced bread

2 tablespoons olive oil, for brushing

cilantro (coriander) leaves, for garnish

Preheat oven to 225°F (110°C/Gas 1/4). Place olive oil, wine, vinegar, sugar, coriander seeds and pepper in a shallow saucepan large enough to hold asparagus. Bring mixture to a boil over medium heat, then reduce heat to low. When mixture is at a steady simmer, add asparagus and cook until tender-crisp, about 5 minutes. Remove asparagus from pan, place in an ovenproof baking dish and keep warm in oven.

Continue to simmer remaining cooking liquid until it has reduced by half, about 5 minutes. Remove asparagus from oven and pour liquid over asparagus.

Preheat a broiler (grill). Brush both sides of bread with olive oil. Broil (grill) until golden, 1–2 minutes per side.

Serve asparagus at room temperature sprinkled with fresh cilantro leaves. Accompany with grilled bread.

Serves 4

ASPARAGUS POACHED IN RED WINE WITH CILANTRO   1 0 5

Glossary

arborio rice: A type of short-grain rice traditionally grown in Italy and used to make risotto. The high starch content of arborio rice gives risotto its characteristic creamy texture.

balsamic vinegar: A rich, strong-flavored, reddish brown vinegar made from unfermented grape juice.

bean sprouts: Sprouted green mung beans, sold fresh or canned. Fresh sprouts have a crisper texture and a more delicate flavor. Store in the refrigerator for up to 3 days.

bok choy: Asian variety of cabbage with thick white stalks and dark green leaves. Sizes of heads vary, from those longer than celery stalks to baby bok choy about 6 inches (15 cm) long. Also known as Chinese cabbage. If unavailable, use Chinese broccoli or choy sum.

chervil: A ferny-leaved herb that resembles parsley and tastes like aniseed. Store up to 1 week in a plastic bag in the refrigerator.

cilantro: Pungent, fragrant leaves from the coriander plant, resembling parsley. Also known as Chinese parsley and coriander. Cilantro (coriander) roots are also used in Asian cooking.

créme fraîche: A cultured cream product with a tangy, tart flavor, similar to sour cream in texture. Substitute sour cream if unavailable.

feta cheese: Greek cheese made from sheep's or goat's milk and stored in brine. Texture of feta ranges from soft and spreadable to hard and crumbly.

fish sauce: Bottled sauce consisting of salted, fermented fish along with other seasonings. Used in moderation to add pungent flavor to dressings, dipping sauces and other Asian recipes. Fish sauces can vary in intensity depending on country of origin. Fish sauce from Thailand, called nam pla, is a commonly available variety.

flat-leaf parsley: Parsley with a flat leaf and a stronger flavor than curly-leaf parsley. Also known as Italian or Continental parsley. Fresh parsley can be stored for up to 1 week in a plastic bag in the refrigerator.

ginger: The thick rootlike rhizome of the ginger plant has a sharp, pungent flavor. Once the thin tan skin is peeled away from fresh ginger, the flesh is grated and used in sauces, marinades, stir-fries and dressings, or is sliced and added to stocks and soups. Store fresh ginger in the refrigerator for up to 3 days.

jasmine rice: A long-grain variety popular in Thailand and appreciated for its sweet aroma and nutty flavor.

kaffir lime leaves: The kaffir lime is a member of the citrus family with leaves that are rich in aromatic oil. Fresh or dried leaves are used whole or shredded to add flavor to Asian dishes.

lemongrass: This tropical grass has pale stalks used to lend an intense lemon flavor to Southeast Asian dishes. Wrap in a damp kitchen towel and store in the refrigerator for up to 1 month. Use grated lemon zest if unavailable.

oyster mushrooms: Creamy white mushrooms with fan-shaped caps, named for their resemblance to an oyster. Possessing a very mild, delicate flavor, oyster mushrooms grow in the wild and are also cultivated. They are available fresh in well-stocked supermarkets and produce markets. Substitute button mushrooms if unavailable.

ricotta cheese: A rich, fresh Italian cheese made from whey left from the production of cheese such as provolone. It is white in color and moist and grainy in texture.

sesame oil, Asian: Dark or golden-colored oil, extracted from sesame seeds, which give it a satisfying, nutty flavor.

shiitake mushrooms: These meaty mushrooms with dark brown caps are available fresh. They are also sold dried and must be reconstituted before use.

soy sauce: Salty sauce made from fermented soybeans, appreciated both as an ingredient and as a table condiment. Dark soy sauce, usually used in cooking, is thicker and often less salty than light soy sauce, which is added to dipping sauces. Low-sodium products are also available.

Thai sweet chili sauce: This mild, sweet chili sauce is used as a flavoring and as a dipping sauce. Store in refrigerator after opening.

Index

Guide to weights and measures

The conversions given in the recipes in this book are approximate. Whichever system you use, remember to follow it consistently, thereby ensuring that the proportions are consistent throughout a recipe.

WEIGHTS

Imperial	Metric
⅓ oz	10 g
½ oz	15 g
¾ oz	20 g
1 oz	30 g
2 oz	60 g
3 oz	90 g
4 oz (¼ lb)	125 g
5 oz (⅓ lb)	150 g
6 oz	180 g
7 oz	220 g
8 oz (½ lb)	250 g
9 oz	280 g
10 oz	300 g
11 oz	330 g
12 oz (¾ lb)	375 g
16 oz (1 lb)	500 g
2 lb	1 kg
3 lb	1.5 kg
4 lb	2 kg

USEFUL CONVERSIONS

¼ teaspoon	1.25 ml
½ teaspoon	2.5 ml
1 teaspoon	5 ml
1 Australian tablespoon	20 ml (4 teaspoons)
1 UK/US tablespoon	15 ml (3 teaspoons)

Butter/Shortening

1 tablespoon	½ oz	15 g
1½ tablespoons	¾ oz	20 g
2 tablespoons	1 oz	30 g
3 tablespoons	1 ½ oz	45 g

OVEN TEMPERATURE GUIDE

The Celsius (°C) and Fahrenheit (°F) temperatures in this chart apply to most electric ovens. Decrease by 25°F or 10°C for a gas oven or refer to the manufacturer's temperature guide. For temperatures below 325°F (160°C), do not decrease the given temperature.

Oven description	°C	°F	Gas Mark
Cool	110	225	¼
	130	250	½
Very slow	140	275	1
	150	300	2
Slow	170	325	3
Moderate	180	350	4
	190	375	5
Moderately Hot	200	400	6
Fairly Hot	220	425	7
Hot	230	450	8
Very Hot	240	475	9
Extremely Hot	250	500	10

VOLUME

Imperial	Metric	Cup
1 fl oz	30 ml	
2 fl oz	60 ml	¼
3	90 ml	⅓
4	125 ml	½
5	150 ml	⅔
6	180 ml	¾
8	250 ml	1
10	300 ml	1¼
12	375 ml	1½
13	400 ml	1⅔
14	440 ml	1¾
16	500 ml	2
24	750 ml	3
32	1L	4

First published in the United States in 2000 by Periplus Editions (HK) Ltd.,
with editorial offices at 153 Milk Street, Boston, Massachusetts 02109 and
5 Little Road #08-01 Singapore 536983

Library of Congress Cataloging-in-Publication Data is available.
ISBN 962-593-821-4

DISTRIBUTED BY

USA
Tuttle Publishing
Distribution Center
Airport Industrial Park
364 Innovation Drive
North Clarendon, VT 05759-9436
Tel: (802) 773-8930
Tel: (800) 526-2778

Japan
Tuttle Publishing
RK Building, 2nd Floor
2-13-10 Shimo-Meguro, Meguro-Ku
Tokyo 153 0064
Tel: (03) 5437-0171
Fax: (03) 5437-0755

Canada
Raincoast Books
8680 Cambie Street
Vancouver, British Colombia
V6P 6M9
Tel: (604) 323 7100
Fax: (604) 323 2600

Southeast Asia
Berkeley Books Pte. Ltd.
5 Little Road #08-01
Singapore 53698
Tel: (65) 280-3320
Fax: (65) 280-6290

Set in Frutiger on QuarkXPress
Printed in Singapore

First Edition
06 05 04 03 02 01 00 10 9 8 7 6 5 4 3 2 1